MIND THE GAP

managing the
space between
your expectations
and reality

TERRIE
CHAPPELL

First published in 2019 by Striving Together Publications, a ministry of Lancaster Baptist Church, Lancaster, CA 93535. Striving Together Publications is committed to providing tried, trusted, and proven resources that will further equip local churches to carry out the Great Commission. Your comments and suggestions are valued.

Striving Together Publications
4020 E. Lancaster Blvd.
Lancaster, CA 93535
800.201.7748
www.strivingtogether.com

Cover design by Andrew Jones
Writing assistance by Anna Gregory

The author and publication team have put forth every effort to give proper credit to quotes and thoughts that are not original with the author. It is not our intent to claim originality with any quote or thought that could not readily be tied to an original source.

ISBN 978-1-59894-404-4
Printed in the United States of America

CONTENTS

INTRODUCTION   v

CHAPTER ONE

Hello Expectations:
Understanding What Expectations Are   1

CHAPTER TWO

From Disappointment to Blessing:
Responding to Unmet Expectations   25

CHAPTER THREE

A Tale of Two Hearts:
Contrasting the Expectations of Mary and Judas   59

CONCLUSION   81

INTRODUCTION

For our twenty-fifth wedding anniversary, my husband and I went to London with our children. It was a special trip that holds some of our favorite family memories.

During our time in London, one phrase in particular became memorable to us all. Whenever we were preparing to board a train or the underground, an automated recording cautioned, "Mind the gap."

The warning refers to the space between the train and the platform. If you overlook it or forget it's there, you may trip and fall.

Like the gap next to the London underground, there is often a gap between our expectations and reality. If we're not aware of it, it can derail our forward progress for God.

For instance, maybe when you were younger, you had expectations of a fairy tale wedding, but you ended up with more of a family-feud marriage. Perhaps you expected that when you had a baby you would have twenty-four-seven "Gerber baby" moments, but you got a baby with colic and who cried nonstop. Or, you might have expected that your annual family vacation would be full of Norman Rockwell moments complete with peace, quiet, tranquility, and happiness. But the whole time, your kids fought in the back seat of the car, you got bug bites, and, to top it off, your car got a flat tire. Perhaps you've gone to church one Sunday morning, excited to hear from God's Word, when you felt a tap on your shoulder from the nursery director. She whispered in your ear, "Hey, I'm so sorry, but we're a little short-staffed—could you help this morning?"

All throughout our lives, we frequently face unmet expectations. And when that happens, we have the choice to either "mind the gap" and not let the unmet expectation distract us or to allow it to derail the rest of our day...or life.

The truth is, we all have thousands of expectations, both big and small, every day. We expect our phones to turn on. We expect water to come out of the faucet. We expect our cars to start. We expect lights to turn on when we flip a switch. We expect to wake up in the morning. We expect to walk outside to sunshine. Without conscious realization, we go throughout our day with thousands of expectations we anticipate to be met.

On a more significant scale, we have expectations about relationships. We expect security with our spouse. We expect our children to obey and love us. We expect our friends to remain loyal. We expect our future to go as we planned—that we'll get that promotion, fall in love, have children, enjoy strong friendships, and our lists go on.

Other people have expectations of us as well. We're expected to show up to work on time. We're expected to take care of our children. We're expected to love our husbands. We're expected to show loyalty to our friends.

Yes, expectations play a huge role in our lives. Because of that, if an expectation isn't met, that reality can hurt or even destroy us. And in our fallen world, unmet expectations are an unfortunate part of our lives.

So what do we do? What happens when our expectations and our reality are mismatched? What do we do when what we thought would happen doesn't? When what we anticipated someone would do is left undone? When the dreams we had for ourselves are unfulfilled? How do we handle unmet expectations?

Through the life of two sisters, Mary and Martha, we're going to explore these questions and discover biblical answers. It turns out that both women had unmet expectations. How they responded—and more importantly how Jesus helped realign their responses—teaches us how we too can wisely manage the unwanted space between our expectations and reality.

CHAPTER ONE

Hello Expectations:
Understanding What Expectations Are

Do you remember Christmas morning when you were a child? You probably woke up early, long before your parents, and ran into the living room, eager to catch a glimpse of what presents might be waiting for you.

Perhaps as you surveyed the presents for the various members of the family, you thought back over the hints you had been dropping since September, trying to guess which present was the right size and shape to be that *one thing* you so desperately wanted.

And then, you saw it—yes, there in the corner. That *had* to be it.

Finally, the time came to open presents. Your fingers flew as you grabbed the present, slipped off the string and bow, ripped away the wrapping paper, and…tried to mask your disappointment. The gift was not at all what you had expected.

I remember a memorable Christmas I had when I was a little girl. My dad wanted to surprise my mom with a sewing machine. He even crafted an elaborate plan to pull off the surprise: he bought the sewing machine, had me wrap it, and put my *brother's* name on the gift. To make sure my mom would be completely surprised, he mentioned to her that he'd bought my brother a train set. What he didn't know, however, was that my brother overheard my dad tell my mom this exciting news about his train set.

Christmas morning came, and my brother was eagerly awaiting his train set. But when he found out that his gift was actually my mom's, he sat back with a hugely disappointed expression on his face. He had been let down by his expectations in a major way.

Whether or not you experienced a Christmas like my brother did, all of us have had those moments of unfulfilled expectations.

We might define expectations as "a strong belief or desire that something will happen or be the case in the future." We could also define them as "a belief that someone will or should achieve something." That "someone" may be you, or it may be another person. Expectations can range from believing you should reach a certain accomplishment by a certain point in your life to anticipating a family member or friend will come through for you in a particular way.

Is having expectations inherently wrong? I don't think it's possible to live without any expectations at all. Our trouble comes when we fail to recognize unrealistic expectations or to respond properly when realistic expectations are not met.

For instance, if you expect that when you have a baby, your church family and neighbors will rally to your side and bring meals for two weeks, do your laundry, and watch your toddlers so you can rest, you may find yourself disillusioned...without ever even realizing that you had an unlikely-to-be-fulfilled expectation.

On the other hand, if you expected your parents to take care of you as a child (a realistic expectation), but instead they neglected or abused you, you may find yourself consumed with bitterness toward your parents. This response to an unfulfilled expectation, even though it was a reasonable expectation, *further* damages you.

In Luke 10, we find a story of unmet expectations. Jesus and His disciples have been traveling, and they come to the home of two sisters and a brother—Mary, Martha, and Lazarus—who welcome them for a meal.

We're going to look at this story as well as a few other incidents in these two sisters' lives as we move through the pages ahead, so take a moment to read it:

> *Now it came to pass, as they went, that he entered into a certain village: and a certain woman named Martha received him into her house. And she had a sister called Mary, which also sat at Jesus' feet, and heard his word. But Martha was cumbered about much serving, and came to him, and said, Lord,*

dost thou not care that my sister hath left me to serve alone? bid her therefore that she help me. And Jesus answered and said unto her, Martha, Martha, thou art careful and troubled about many things: But one thing is needful: and Mary hath chosen that good part, which shall not be taken away from her.—LUKE 10:38–42

Picture Martha, trying to prepare a meal for her guests, looking over to see her sister sitting at the feet of Jesus. I can almost see her walking into the room where Mary, Jesus, and the disciples were, her hand on one hip, mixing bowl in the other, a little flour on her cheek, and flyaway hairs sticking out because of the heat of the kitchen. I can imagine her taking in the scene, giving Mary a significant look, and pointedly saying to Jesus, "Lord, dost thou not care that my sister hath left me to serve alone? Bid her therefore that she help me!"

Can you say, "Hello, expectations"?

As I read this story, I can hear a tone in Martha's voice that I've heard too often in my own. It's not a tone of kindness and hospitality; it's that tone of frustrated expectations. She was all at once saying to Mary, "Can't you see I need help?" and to Jesus, "Don't you care about the work I'm doing for You?"

In our own minds, our expectations are obvious, and they are *right*.

But Jesus rebuked Martha, letting her know that her expectation of Mary was a faulty one. He told Martha that Mary was right to be where she was and doing what she was doing.

Before we look specifically at how Jesus helped Martha deal with her unmet expectation in our next chapter, let's notice a few characteristics of expectations themselves…and what happens in our lives if we fail to deal with unmet expectations properly. Perhaps as you read through these characteristics, you'll identify a previously unrecognized expectation in your own life.

Expectations come in all shapes and sizes.

Expectations, just like the people who have them, come in all shapes and sizes. In fact, you probably have at least one hundred expectations every day. This morning, for example, when you brushed your teeth, you probably expected water to come out of the faucet. When you put the key in the ignition of your car to drive to work, you likely expected the car to start. We expect the sun to rise every morning. Large, small, realistic, unrealistic, helpful, hurtful, inspiring, tiring…expectations, in all forms, permeate our day-to-day lives.

We have good expectations and not-so-good expectations. For example, you probably expect your children to obey. (That's a good expectation.) At the same time, however, we can put pressure on our children to do something or be someone that God doesn't even expect of them.

We have realistic expectations and unrealistic expectations. We might convince ourselves that we can clean our home in forty-five minutes. And, three hours later, staring at a finally-clean home, we realize that our expectations might have been a little ambitious.

We all experience unmet expectations.

Although some of our expectations will be met, some of them will not. To those around us, our unmet expectation might not be a big deal. But to us, an unmet expectation can be devastating.

Winnie the Pooh once said, "Sometimes the smallest things take up the most space in your heart." We smile at this statement, but when it comes to unmet expectations, it's painfully true. When your expectation isn't fulfilled, it hurts. Every woman has a desire for her expectations to be met, no matter how strong and unfazed she appears outwardly.

But how we respond to these unmet expectations has a powerful effect on the rest of our lives—for good or for bad. I remember a few years ago stopping by a hardware store to pick out paint samples. By coincidence, I met a young woman, about twenty-six years old, who was a Christian. As we began talking, she shared with me how, two years ago, her husband died at age twenty-four of a brain aneurism. I can only imagine that on her wedding day, she had the expectation of growing old with her husband. Her choice to have joy, however, despite the trial she walked through, was an incredible testimony to me of responding correctly to unmet expectations.

Perhaps you're thinking of a different unmet expectation in your life. Maybe you've been married for several years. You had planned to have a child soon after you were married, but ten years have passed and you're still childless.

Maybe you do have children. You expected them to have a happy childhood, go to college, establish themselves with successful careers, and love and serve God with their lives. Instead, however, they were born with special needs. Or maybe they were diagnosed with cancer a few months after they were born. As you watch them endure chemo treatments, you ask yourself why God would let you walk through this trial.

Our tendency during a season of unmet expectation is to be consumed with thoughts of ourselves and how hard we have it. The reality is, however, that every person on earth has unmet expectations and the hurt and pain that come with them. Often, God desires to use us to be a blessing to others during their seasons of difficulty.

We expect the most from those we love and those who love us.

When we love someone or believe they love us, we often place higher expectations on that person.

As you were growing up, you likely placed your strongest expectations on your parents. You expected that they would provide for your needs and give you emotional support and guidance.

If you are married, from the time of your wedding, you expected your husband to fulfill a large portion of your emotional, physical, and spiritual needs. You love and trust your husband and have placed expectations on him. You likely have certain expectations from close friends or your children. You love them, and they love you in return.

What happens, then, when our expectations aren't met by someone we love? Maybe we prayed about something for a long time, but when God answers "no," we tell ourselves, "If God *really* loved me, He would . . ." Or, "If God actually cared about me, this wouldn't have happened."

Perhaps we trusted a leader we loved or a family member, but that person let us down. Our expectations were shattered. Somehow, because we trusted that person, those unmet expectations hurt even more.

We assume our expectations will be met.

Okay, this one seems obvious, but it's still important to recognize that expectations are, after all, simply an assumption on our part.

Have you ever said (or thought), "I want what I want and I want it now"? Although we might phrase it more graciously, all of us have had that attitude. We simply assume our expectations will be met.

This is why it is so important that we identify our expectations. When we hear ourselves saying, "But I thought…" we can know we had an expectation that things would go differently.

If we recognize something as an expectation, we're better able to determine if it is based on pure motives and something we should work toward, or if it is selfish and something we should set aside. We're able to determine if it is realistic and something we should communicate to those around us, or if it is unrealistic and is causing us to put undue pressure on our relationships.

Not all expectations are wrong. Throughout the Bible, we see verses that encourage us to have expectations and expect them to be met. Look at Proverbs 22:6. "Train up a child in the way he should go: and when he is old, he will not depart from it." We are to expect that, if we train our children to love God, they will after they leave the house.

Philippians 1:20 tells us, "According to my earnest expectation and my hope, that in nothing I shall be ashamed, but that with all boldness, as always, so now also Christ shall be magnified in my body, whether it be by life, or by death." This verse encourages us to give our lives fully to the Lord, expecting that He is magnified through our sacrifices for Him.

Jeremiah 33:3 states, "Call unto me, and I will answer thee, and show thee great and mighty things, which though knowest not." We need to call on the Lord, expecting Him to do great things in our lives.

But when we sense the disappointment of an unmet expectation, we need to step back and evaluate, *Was this just something I assumed I deserved? Or is this a legitimate need I need to wait on God to fulfill?*

We often respond to unmet expectations by quitting.

What happens when our expectations aren't met? The easiest thing to do is to quit—just walk away from that relationship or difficulty. Or perhaps we can't walk away, but we just quit in our hearts, investing no further energy or effort into change. We tell ourselves, "My expectations won't be met—why even bother? I don't want to be hurt anymore. I give up." But giving up because of an unmet expectation is like the old expression puts it: throwing the baby out with the bathwater.

One of my favorite verses in the Bible is Ephesians 3:20, which reads, "Now unto him that is able to do exceeding abundantly above all that we ask or think according to the power that worketh in us." Did you catch that? Not only are we to expect God to do great things, we're to expect him to *exceed* our expectations.

If not dealt with properly, we will experience the manifestations of unmet expectations.

I once heard someone say, "Expectation is the mother of all frustration." If we don't deal with unmet expectations properly, that statement is absolutely true.

There are actually several pitfalls of unmet expectations. Let's look at a few:

Disappointment—The first way frustration over an unmet expectation often shows itself is through disappointment. The Bible tells us, "Hope deferred maketh the heart sick: but when the desire cometh, it is a tree of life" (Proverbs 13:12).

Just like a tree begins to grow when a seed is planted in the ground, an expectation begins to grow when its seed is planted in our minds. If, however, that expectation doesn't come to fruition, it's easy to become disappointed. We *thought* something would happen, but it didn't. That void leaves us disappointed.

When my daughter Kristine was young, our family was playing a rousing round of Monopoly. Although she was just a little too young to be playing, she wanted to be part of the action. Not surprisingly, she lost the game. As we were nearing the end, she finally looked at my husband and said, "I'm not mad, I'm not sad, I'm just a little disappointed." To this day, we still tease her about that statement. She had an expectation of winning, and, when that didn't happen, she wasn't mad, she wasn't sad, she was just a little disappointed.

Has your husband ever told you early in the week, "This Friday, I'm going to take you out to dinner." All week, you plan the evening out in your mind. *I'll sit down to cloth napkins and a perfectly set table. Classical music will play in the background, provided by a live orchestra. They'll serve perfectly seasoned Italian food. Candles will be lit on each table . . .*

But what if Friday came and your husband took you to Taco Bell? You'd likely be a little disappointed—not because your husband didn't keep his word, but because of a faulty expectation on your part.

Assumptions—Unmet expectations don't just stop at disappointment. Often, our disappointment leads to assumptions about someone's character.

We think, "If he really loved me, he would . . ." Or, "I bet she forgot about this because…" Although it's easy to jump to conclusions about something or someone, it's a wrong response and leads to hurt in relationships.

Proverbs 18:2 tells us, "A fool hath no delight in understanding, but that his heart may discover itself." Essentially, when we don't seek to understand a matter, we're acting like fools. Instead of jumping to conclusions about why someone didn't do something we expected, we should seek to understand. When we jump to assumptions and fail to give someone the benefit of the doubt, we can destroy a relationship.

Anger—Another way unmet expectations show themselves in our lives is through anger. Remember Naaman? He had leprosy and expected Elisha to heal him in a dramatic moment of power. But when Elisha instead gave Naaman a simple instruction—go wash seven times in the Jordan River, Naaman was angry. Second Kings 5:11–12 relates the story: "But Naaman was wroth, and went away, and said, Behold, I thought, He will surely come out to me, and stand, and call on the name of the Lord his God, and strike his hand over the place, and recover the leper. Are not Abana and Pharpar, rivers of Damascus, better than all the waters of Israel? may I not wash in them, and be clean? So he turned and went away in a rage."

Sometimes, we think that, as long as we don't really show our anger, it's not a big deal. But anger, even in the smallest form, can end up destroying us. Mark Twain once aptly said, "Anger is an acid that can do more harm to the vessel in which it is stored than to anything on which it is poured."

At times, it can be hard to know if we've truly forgiven someone. We think that we've let go of some unmet expectation, but each time we think about another's actions, we get angry. A test to see if we've truly forgiven someone is to see if we can think about an incident without growing angry. If we can, it's likely that we've forgiven that person.

The Bible repeatedly encourages us to flee from anger. Psalm 37:8 says, "Cease from anger, and forsake wrath: fret not thyself in any wise to do evil." James 1:20 states, "For the wrath of man worketh not the righteousness of God."

As we go through our lives, people are going to do things to us that hurt us, and sometimes deeply. And while there is real pain involved in that, when we choose to overlook a transgression, the Bible describes it as a glory. Proverbs 19:11 says, "The discretion of a man deferreth his anger; and it is his glory to pass over a transgression."

The Lord revealed to us the greatest example of mercy when He chose to forgive our transgressions. Psalm 103:8 reminds us, "The Lord is merciful and gracious, slow to anger, and plenteous in mercy." If we're saved, we're redeemed, but we still have our fallen nature. The Lord, however, is slow to anger and chooses to overlook our transgressions when we run to Him for forgiveness.

We, too, can learn to respond to disappointing situations with grace instead of with anger.

Bitterness—If someone doesn't meet our expectations, it's easy for us to replay what happened to us over and over in our minds, and this leads to bitterness.

Because that person didn't do what we thought they should do, we grow bitter. Because that church didn't satisfy what we were wanting, we grow bitter. Because that relationship didn't end the way we expected, we grow bitter.

The problem with bitterness is that we can't expect to be bitter but have our lives sweet. Ephesians 4:32 instructs, "And be ye kind one to another, tenderhearted, forgiving one another, even as God for Christ's sake hath forgiven you."

One of the secrets to a joy-filled life is choosing to give grace rather than being filled with bitterness.

Leaving the Will of God—Another manifestation of unmet expectations is making poor choices outside the will of God. Remember Abraham and Sarah? God promised Abraham that he would be the father of a great nation. But when Sarah passed her fiftieth, sixtieth, seventieth, eightieth, and ninetieth birthday, I think it would have been easy to start to doubt God's promise. Talk about unmet expectations!

Sarah decided to take matters into her own hands and gave her handmaid to her husband. Sarah, I'm sure, felt that by providing another way for Abraham to have a child, she was helping God out. What she failed to realize is that God doesn't need our assistance.

Something similar happened in the life of the Israelite King Saul. He was preparing for battle, and the prophet Samuel had instructed Saul to wait until Samuel came and offered a sacrifice.

Samuel didn't come as soon as Saul expected, so Saul took matters into his own hands and offered the sacrifice himself, which under Old Testament law, he was not to have done. When Samuel arrived, he rebuked Saul for leaving God's will to hurry things up:

"And Samuel said to Saul, Thou hast done foolishly: thou hast not kept the commandment of the Lord thy God, which he commanded thee: for now would the Lord have established thy kingdom upon Israel for ever. But now thy kingdom shall not continue…" (1 Samuel 13:13–14).

When our expectations aren't met by God the moment we expect them to be, we shouldn't take control of the situation. Instead, we need to step back and trust God and His timetable. "Rest in the LORD, and wait patiently for him…" (Psalm 37:7).

A Hardened Heart—When we make poor choices outside of the will of God, we begin, often imperceptibly at first, to harden our hearts. Because of our unmet expectations, we close our hearts to God's Word and the hope He gives. We're slowly drawn away from the Lord and His desires for us.

A hard heart actually leads to unbelief. This is what happened to the Israelites as God led them across the wilderness to the Promised Land. Even though God worked miracle after miracle for their deliverance and provision, they constantly complained because things weren't the way they expected.

When they reached the edge of the land God had promised them, their hardened, faithless hearts refused to believe that God could help them conquer the giants who lived there. As a result of their hardened hearts, they did not get to go in. Using their example, Psalm 95:7–8 warns us, "…To day if ye will hear his voice, Harden not your heart, as in the provocation, and as in the day of temptation in the wilderness."

When we become fixated on how we think God should act on our behalf—and then He doesn't follow our plans—we slowly harden our hearts toward God in unbelief. Ultimately, we then miss out on God's better plan.

None of us want to live with unmet expectations. But even worse than an unrealized expectation is the consequences of not dealing with it properly. Disappointment, assumptions, anger, bitterness, leaving God's will, a hardened heart—none of these are what we want to experience in our lives.

So how *do* we deal with unmet expectations? We learn that from Jesus' counsel to Martha.

CHAPTER TWO

From Disappointment to Blessing: Responding to Unmet Expectations

I have no problem admitting that I am not a shopper. In fact, when I find services that eliminate the need for me to go into a store, I probably get a little too excited. That's why Walmart pickup has become my new best friend. I simply place my grocery order online, and the order is brought out to my car. Occasionally, Walmart will be out of what I order, and they'll provide substitutions. Usually, the substitutions are even better. For example, one time, I needed eighteen eggs. Walmart was out of the eighteen eggs carton, so they brought me two dozen.

I remember one time I was having company over and had placed an order through Walmart pickup. One of the items I needed was fresh basil for the basil caprese salad I was making. When I went to pick up my order, the woman who had brought my order to the car explained that the store was out of fresh basil.

She told me that they had dried basil as a substitution, but if you know anything about a basil caprese salad, you know that you *have* to have fresh basil. I told the lady that I couldn't use dried basil. I was frustrated, not at the lady, but at the fact that I'd have to spend time I didn't really have to hunt down fresh basil at another store.

My disappointment turned to joy, however, when the employee brought out a fresh plant of basil. Not only did I have the ingredient that I needed, I had a fresh basil plant. At first, I was frustrated because my expectation wasn't met. But then, my expectation was exceeded.

On a far larger scale, that's what God wants to do with our unmet expectations. He wants to take our disappointments and transform them into blessings that exceed our hopes. This takes place through a process of yielding to the Lord, bringing our broken dreams to Him, waiting on Him, and letting Him change *us* as He works in ways we cannot.

In our previous chapter, we saw our friend Martha facing an unmet expectation as her sister Mary sat at Jesus' feet listening and learning rather than helping Martha in the kitchen. Martha stormed in to complain to Christ about the unfairness of the situation.

Through Martha's frustration and Christ's response, we learn six steps to dealing with unmet expectations.

Beware of the Idol of Self

"Lord, dost thou not care…?"

When Martha saw Jesus allowing Mary to linger in fellowship with Him, she made a quick judgment: "But Martha was cumbered about much serving, and came to him, and said, Lord, *dost thou not care* that my sister hath left me to serve alone? bid her therefore that she help me."

Have you ever said something like that? Maybe you've said to your husband, "You don't care that I've been home all day with the kids doing laundry and dishes." Maybe you've insisted, "You don't care that I had to go through this today." Or maybe you remember blurting out as a teenager, "Mom and Dad, you don't care about me anymore and what I'm going through!"

During the first year my husband and I were married, he was invited to a preacher's conference. That first year of ministry as a new couple on staff, we were very tight on money. In fact, at that point we didn't have any food in the house. My expectation of my husband's time at the conference was that my husband would be away, feasting with other pastors, while I stayed home hungry. I started thinking, "What am I going to do?" My back-up plan, in all honesty, was to visit my mom for dinner.

As my husband prepared to leave, I blurted out, "You don't care about me. You're going off to this big conference leaving me at home with nothing to eat."

Instead of saying anything, my husband got on his knees and began praying for God's provision. I thought, *We should have been on our knees praying all week, but here you are leaving in a couple of hours.* It was wrong of me, but I just wasn't in the mood to pray. Instead, I just stood there.

In the middle of my husband's prayer, the phone rang. Since I wasn't doing anything at the time, I walked over to answer it. On the other end was a pastor my husband had preached for a few months back. He asked to speak to my husband.

I could only overhear snippets of the conversation. My husband would say things like, "Oh no, you don't have to do that" and "It really doesn't matter." Finally, he hung up the phone and explained.

"The pastor said that he'd never given me a love gift or an honorarium for my preaching," my husband began. "He wants to follow up on that, and the Lord impressed on his heart to drive down with the money right now."

The pastor drove down and gave my husband a $100 bill, which my husband promptly handed to me. At this point, I was in tears. The Lord had answered my husband's prayer in a tangible way, but I had first accused my husband (and perhaps subconsciously the Lord as well) of not caring about my needs.

In the moment of an unmet expectation, it's easy to blurt out to God or to someone else, "You don't care about me." But, when we make statements like that, do you see where our focus lies? Our focus is placed on ourselves. Instead of focusing on the needs of others, we only focus on our needs.

Do you hear any mention in Martha's accusation of care for Mary and *her* spiritual renewal? Or of care for Jesus and gladness that He could receive Mary's attention and worship?

Truly, I can sympathize with Martha's feelings. I would guess that she wanted to sit with Jesus also, but she needed to accomplish some things in the kitchen. When she looked out and saw Mary sitting at the feet of Jesus, she grew frustrated. She probably thought, *Mary, seriously? If you'd just help me in the kitchen, we'd finish in half the time. Then, we'd both be able to sit with Jesus.*

Martha had an expectation of what Mary should do, and she imposed that expectation on Mary. In a world that is constantly fixating on self, it's easy to get caught up in that idol of selfishness.

How do we get ourselves in positions like this? How do we get so focused on ourselves that we can get sidelined when our expectations aren't met? How do we battle this idol of self?

From a practical perspective, it helps to communicate. We often have expectations that others would be happy to help meet, but we have not clearly communicated them.

This is a little bit of conjuncture, but it seems that Martha had not previously communicated her expectation for help to Mary. (Remember, one challenge of expectations is that they are so obvious to us that we don't even recognize them as an expectation, but just assume others will see them the way we do.)

I remember one particular instance when this happened to me years ago. Our children were small, and my husband and I discussed planning a special family day after a particularly busy season of ministry. He offhandedly mentioned going to Sea World in San Diego. I thought that sounded great and began to assume that we were definitely going to Sea World. Every time this family day came up, my expectation grew. Although my husband never actually brought up Sea World again to me and I never confirmed with him that was where we were going, in my mind, the deal was done.

The day came, and we began traveling toward San Diego. In the car, I was already picturing the food I was going to eat, shows I was going to watch, and exhibits we would enjoy with the children. My expectations and excitement were growing by the second.

Finally, we took the exit...but the exit didn't look exactly like what I thought the Sea World exit would look. Then, I saw a sign for the San Diego Zoo. My heart sank when I realized that we weren't going to Sea World—we were going to the San Diego Zoo.

Don't get me wrong; I enjoy the zoo. But after weeks of looking forward to Sea World, I was disappointed.

My disappointment in that unmet expectation wasn't my husband's fault. It was my fault for not communicating clearly. People can't read our thought bubbles. Unless we tell them what we're thinking, they won't know.

As a mom, I've learned over the years the importance of making sure that my kids know what to expect from me. In our minds as parents, we think we've been overly clear to our children, but when they do the opposite of what we asked—or what we thought we asked—we grow frustrated.

We have no problem communicating what they did wrong after the fact, but we often don't communicate what's expected in advance. In reality, we can't *expect* what we don't *express*. The next time you have an unmet expectation, ask yourself, "Did I communicate clearly? Would this person have understood what my expectation was?"

Communicating clearly does help avoid some unmet expectations, and Martha could have done better here.

But once we are past that opportunity for prior communication, the frustration we feel in our unmet expectations has a way of revealing our idol of self. In that moment, we need to choose to die to self.

Although Martha had the wrong expectation, at least she took her expectation to the Lord. We need to do the same…but not in the way that Martha did. Instead of accusing Him of not caring about us, we should bring our needs to the Lord with an attitude of surrender. Our hearts should be, "Lord, I give all of my expectations to You. I want You to do with them as You desire. I'm choosing to die to myself."

The apostle Paul's testimony in Galatians 2:20 should be ours as well: "I am crucified with Christ: nevertheless I live; yet not I, but Christ liveth in me: and the life which I now live in the flesh I live by the faith of the Son of God, who loved me, and gave himself for me."

When we die to self, we no longer have this need to have something our way. We simply choose to want what the Lord wants. Gary Thomas, author of *Sacred Marriage*, said, "Each day we must die to our own desires and rise as a servant. Each day we are called to identify with the suffering Christ on the cross, and then be empowered by the resurrected Christ. We die to our expectations, our demands, and our fears. We rise to compromise, service, and courage."

My husband and I have noticed in marriage counseling that the number one complaint we hear is, "My needs aren't being met," *not*, "I'm not meeting my husband's/wife's needs." In any relationship, it's so easy for our focus to be on our own needs, rather than on the needs of the other person.

The idol of self easily sneaks into our lives, pulling us away from what the Lord wants for us. If we are to win over unmet expectations, we must beware of this pride.

Battle to Keep Focus

"...that my sister hath left me to serve alone? bid her therefore that she help me."

Let's look back to Martha again: "But Martha was cumbered about much serving, and came to him, and said, Lord, dost thou not care that my sister hath left me to serve alone? Bid her therefore that she help me."

Where was Martha's focus? On herself, yes, but it was also on her sister and what she was *not* doing. Instead of Martha being able to just remain focused on the job in front of her, her thoughts were consumed with Mary's lack of help. When Martha saw Mary relaxing at Jesus' feet while she herself was working hard, she grew discouraged and perhaps jealous.

Many of us relate. Maybe it's been a long day and your husband comes home, props his feet up, and relaxes in the recliner. You see that as you're trying to clean mounds of dishes and fold laundry after a long day of watching the kids, helping with homework, and cooking three meals. You're tired, and you want to put your feet up too. And somehow, having someone else nearby relaxing makes the same tasks you were doing earlier feel heavier.

At work, we may notice others who aren't helping us in ways that they could. In ministry, we might look at all the women who *don't* serve in the nursery or help in a Sunday school class.

Our focus, however, shouldn't be on what others are not doing. Our focus should be on whether or not we're doing everything that we can do to serve the Lord and be faithful in the responsibilities He has given to us.

When we have an unmet expectation, we can become professional blame shifters. Instead of looking to what we should be doing, we blame others for what they are not doing. Martha looked at Mary and was convinced that the reason dinner wasn't getting on the table faster was because Mary wasn't helping. Martha freely expressed her opinions to the Lord.

When I think of this story, I have to smile, at least a little. Martha was so concerned about preparing a meal that she forgot she was sitting with the Creator of the Universe. With a spoken word, Jesus could have created a meal and eliminated the issue Martha was so worried about.

When our focus is off the Lord, we open our hearts to bitterness. We can become bitter that someone didn't help in the way we thought they should, that someone's having an easier time of it than we are, that another woman can have children and we can't, that another woman is married and we're still single, that our neighbor has a wonderful marriage while ours is struggling. The pain of unmet expectations is fueled by comparison.

If we continue to compare, mulling over the what-ifs and hurts in our minds, we will grow bitter. It may not happen in a week, a month, or even a year. But if our focus is not on Christ, we have opened the door to bitterness.

Instead of bitterness, God calls us to forgive. "Let all bitterness, and wrath, and anger, and clamour, and evil speaking, be put away from you, with all malice: And be ye kind one to another, tenderhearted, forgiving one another, even as God for Christ's sake hath forgiven you" (Ephesians 4:31–32).

When we make the daily choice to die to self and place our focus on Christ, it becomes easier to overlook the shortcomings of others.

I don't think that Martha walked away from her experience as a bitter person. In John 12, we see another glimpse into the story of Mary, Martha, and their brother Lazarus.

> *Then Jesus six days before the passover came to Bethany, where Lazarus was, which had been dead, whom he raised from the dead. There they made him a supper; and Martha served: but Lazarus was one of them that sat at the table with him.*— JOHN 12:1–2

Here, Jesus is with His disciples again at Mary and Martha's house. Martha is still serving the Lord. I have to think that, had she grown bitter, she wouldn't have continued to serve the Lord joyfully. Based on this later passage, I think that Martha began to recognize the importance of worshipping at Jesus' feet like Mary.

Worship God with Intensity

"…but one thing is needful…"

Mary recognized the importance of worship, and Jesus commended her for her devotion to Him. "But one thing is needful: and Mary hath chosen that good part, which shall not be taken away from her."

This was the opposite of what Martha expected to hear from the Lord. She probably thought that Jesus would tell Mary to help her, but He didn't. The Lord knew that Martha needed to simply sit at His feet.

Micah 6:8 tells us, "He hath shewed thee, O man, what is good; and what doth the Lord require of thee, but to do justly, and to love mercy, and to walk humbly with thy God?" These are powerful words! We will never lose by spending time with the Lord and walking with Him. In fact, we gain a fresh perspective and renewed joy when we spend time at the feet of Jesus.

If you're struggling with an unmet expectation, choose to worship the Lord. As you go throughout your day, sing hymns of praise. Meditate on a passage of Scripture. Praise God for who He is to you. Pick one of the Lord's attributes, and focus on it.

Instead of thinking about the Lord, we want to replay that unmet expectation to the point that it steals our joy. We have to choose, however, to worship the Lord intentionally. When we do, our focus is automatically realigned with the Lord and His incredible plan for our lives.

Accept What God Wants You to Experience

". . . and Mary hath chosen that good part . . ."

All of us have an idea of what our ideal life would look like. But if you've been saved for very long, you've likely realized that God's plans are often different from your own. In truth, God's plans are better than ours, but we often do not have the perspective to be able to see it.

Part of battling an unmet expectation is simply accepting what God wants us to experience—in Martha's case, to learn the importance of worshipping at Jesus feet. But what do we tend to do when something unexpected comes into our lives? We try to push the obstacle away. Although we might not express it in this way, we're opinionated about what we think God should do in our lives.

If the Lord loved me, we think, *this wouldn't happen.* Or, *God should fix _____ in my life.*

Sometimes, however, God *allows* difficulty in our lives to make us more like Him. I think of people throughout the Bible who experienced unmet expectations. I'm sure that Esther never expected to be forced into marriage with a heathen king, yet God used that experience in her life to save the Jewish people. I doubt Ruth ever expected to end up gleaning in a field in a foreign land, yet God used that experience to place her in the lineage of Christ.

Throughout our lives, we are going to walk through things that are difficult. As we grow through those difficult times, we need God's grace. And we need to realize that, even when we don't understand, God has a purpose. In every trial, He has something for us to learn.

What Jesus had in mind was not that Martha would do the work for Jesus, but that Jesus would do a work in Martha.

This was true also in another experience in these sisters' lives that related to a great need and an unmet expectation. As we work through the final three steps of dealing with unmet expectations, notice how these two stories—Mary and Martha at dinner time and Mary and Martha when their brother becomes ill and dies—parallel in the truths they teach us.

> *Now a certain man was sick, named Lazarus, of Bethany, the town of Mary and her sister Martha. (It was that Mary which anointed the Lord with ointment, and wiped his feet with her hair, whose brother Lazarus was sick.) Therefore his sisters sent unto him, saying, Lord, behold, he whom thou lovest is sick. When Jesus heard that, he said, This sickness is not unto death, but for the glory of God, that the Son of God might be glorified thereby. Now Jesus loved Martha, and her sister, and Lazarus. When he had heard therefore that he was sick, he*

abode two days still in the same place where he
was.—JOHN 11:1–6

In this passage, Mary and Martha had an expectation that Jesus would immediately come to heal their brother. Remember, they didn't know the ending of the story like we do. All they knew was that their brother was extremely ill and desperately needed Jesus' healing touch.

This expectation that Jesus would come heal their brother would be a natural thought for them. After all, if you go back and read the verses in the previous chapter, you see Jesus healing many people. They had heard about Jesus performing these miracles and expected Jesus to come. In fact, they would have probably thought that when Jesus heard of their need, He would drop everything to come heal Lazarus, whom He loved. Perhaps they were even expecting Jesus to heal Lazarus from a distance, with just His word, as He did for the centurion's servant (Matthew 8:13).

But that's not at all what happened. Even though Jesus knew Lazarus was sick, He chose to stay for two more days. Before Jesus finally arrived, Lazarus had already died.

So often we expect God to do something for us immediately, and when He doesn't, we become disappointed in Him. But the fact that God didn't do what we expected doesn't mean that He has forgotten about us. After all, God's delays are not God's denials. It simply means that He has something better in mind. He can see things in the future that we can't. And when He says "no" to an earnest prayer request from one of His children, it's because He has an even better plan.

We can rest confidently in the truth that God's plan is always best. He assures us, "For I know the thoughts that I think toward you, saith the Lord, thoughts of peace, and not of evil, to give you an expected end" (Jeremiah 29:11). Pause and think about that in relation to your unmet expectation. God's plan is always the best. He always has thoughts of peace toward you. He loves you. He is in control.

Keep an Eternal Perspective

"…which shall not be taken away from her."

Throughout our lives, we're going to walk through things we don't understand. Our lives can be turned upside down with just one trip to a doctor or an unexpected phone call. When we walk through those tough times, our first inclination is often to ask God, "Why? Why are You letting me go through this? Why don't You make it all stop?"

When you wake up in the morning, it's likely that you aren't *expecting* something bad to happen that day. In fact, you probably run through a mental checklist of all the things you need to accomplish. But then an unexpected trial comes, it's difficult to remember that God has another perspective than we do.

I love these comforting words from Isaiah 55:8–9, "For my thoughts are not your thoughts, neither are your ways my ways, saith the LORD. For as the heavens are higher than the earth, so are my ways higher than your ways, and my thoughts than your thoughts."

We may think that our plan is better. Sometimes, we have our prayers planned out the way we think they should be answered. But when our prayers *aren't* answered the way we anticipated, we have to rest in who God is, keeping an eternal perspective, even in the middle of our pain.

This heavenly perspective was what Mary was absorbing by sitting at Jesus' feet that day He came to dinner. But when Lazarus was sick and then died, both Mary and Martha struggled to keep that heavenly perspective. And they weren't the only ones. Jesus' disciples faced this struggle too.

Let's look at the story again. This picks up when Jesus was telling His disciples that He was now preparing to go to this family He loved.

> *These things said he: and after that he saith unto them, Our friend Lazarus sleepeth; but I go, that I may awake him out of sleep. Then said his disciples, Lord, if he sleep, he shall do well. Howbeit Jesus spake of his death: but they thought that he had spoken of taking of rest in sleep. Then said Jesus*

unto them plainly, Lazarus is dead. And I am glad
for your sakes that I was not there, to the intent ye
may believe; nevertheless let us go unto him. Then
said Thomas, which is called Didymus, unto his
fellowdisciples, Let us also go, that we may die with
him.—JOHN 11:11–16

The disciples thought that Lazarus was on the
mend because he was sleeping. They didn't realize
until Jesus clearly told them that Lazarus was dead.
Even then, Thomas had the wrong perspective. He
thought that they were basically taking a suicide trip
down to see Mary and Martha.

We'll look at the miraculous outcome of Lazarus'
story in just a moment, but can you sympathize with
Thomas and the rest of the disciples? In the middle
of a confusing time, we too tend to focus on what
is wrong.

Maintaining a heavenly perspective reminds us,
however, that we can trust that the One who created
the universe has a perfect plan for our lives. J. Vernon
McGee once said, "This is God's universe, and God
does things his way. You may have a better way, but

you don't have a universe." I love that thought. Because God created all things, He understands our needs better than we do.

I grew up in an unsaved family and was led to Christ through the children's outreach of a local Baptist church. As I grew in the Lord, I remember many times looking at my friends who did live in saved homes and asking God, "Why didn't you just put me in a saved family home? My parents won't even let me go to church sometimes."

Looking back, however, I'm so thankful for my past. Yes, it was difficult at the time. But my experience has helped me so much to sympathize with others. It has helped me to make sure that my walk with the Lord was founded on my personal convictions, not necessarily just what I grew up with.

Every day, we must choose to trust God with both our past and our future. You see, we can't control our future; only God can. We can't change our past. All we can do is choose to focus on truth—that God has a perfect plan for our lives and we can trust Him. When you're in the middle of a confusing time, trust

God. Don't quit. Whatever the gap is between your expectation and the reality of your present, make the choice to trust God.

Whatever circumstance God has you in, trust Him. He has a great plan for you that is much greater than you will ever know. Even when our expectations *aren't* met, we can trust that God has an even better plan.

Live to Glorify God

"This sickness is not unto death,
but for the glory of God…"

What Mary and Martha could not see in their disappointment and grief as Jesus didn't fulfill their expectation to heal Lazarus, was that Jesus had a greater purpose—one that would far exceed their expectations. John 11:4 states: "When Jesus heard that, he said, This sickness is not unto death, *but for the glory of God*, that the Son of God might be glorified thereby."

Did you catch that? Jesus knew that raising Lazarus back to life would bring Him more glory than simply healing Lazarus. Jesus chose not to meet Mary and Martha's expectation immediately because He had a bigger picture in mind: to glorify God. Let's look at the rest of the story.

> *Jesus saith unto her, Said I not unto thee, that, if thou wouldest believe, thou shouldest see the glory of God? Then they took away the stone from the place where the dead was laid. And Jesus lifted up his eyes, and said, Father, I thank thee that thou hast heard me. And I knew that thou hearest me always: but because of the people which stand by I said it, that they may believe that thou hast sent me. And when he thus had spoken, he cried with a loud voice, Lazarus, come forth. And he that was dead came forth, bound hand and foot with graveclothes: and his face was bound about with a napkin. Jesus saith unto them, Loose him, and let him go. Then many of the Jews which came to Mary, and had seen the things which Jesus did, believed on him.—JOHN 11:40–45*

Truly, God demonstrated that He could not just meet but *exceed* expectations that day. He raised a man *from the dead!* Ultimately, God was glorified through the difficulty of an unmet expectation.

When our expectations are not met, we have to recognize that God has a bigger and better plan, and we need to choose to live to bring God glory.

Perhaps you remember the story of the lame man begging in Acts 3. He saw Peter and John and expected them to give him money. They didn't, but they gave him something so much better.

> *Now Peter and John went up together into the temple at the hour of prayer, being the ninth hour. And a certain man lame from his mother's womb was carried, whom they laid daily at the gate of the temple which is called Beautiful, to ask alms of them that entered into the temple; Who seeing Peter and John about to go into the temple asked an alms. And Peter, fastening his eyes upon him with John, said, Look on us. And he gave heed unto them, expecting to receive something of them. Then Peter said, Silver and gold have I none; but such*

as I have give I thee: In the name of Jesus Christ
of Nazareth rise up and walk. And he took him by
the right hand, and lifted him up: and immediately
his feet and ankle bones received strength.
—ACTS 3:1–7

Can you imagine all that this lame man must have felt? At first, he was probably disappointed. He wanted money, but Peter and John didn't have any to give. Instead of receiving money, however, he was healed. If you read the rest of the chapter, this man immediately began to praise God in front of all the people. God received the glory through this man's unmet expectations.

Like He did for the lame man, God wants to exceed our expectations. Ephesians 3:20 says, "Now unto him that is able to do exceeding abundantly above all that we ask or think, according to the power that worketh in us."

The first verse I memorized after becoming a Christian was 1 Corinthians 10:31. "Whether therefore ye eat, or drink, or whatsoever ye do, do all to the glory of God." All that we do should be done for God's glory. When God brings into your life a circumstance that is not your expectation, you can trust Him.

This brings us full circle, doesn't it? In fact, choosing to die to self (the first step we looked at) is really how we live to God's glory. Rather than demanding our expectations be met (as Martha began), we surrender in order that Christ might receive glory from our lives. And even when we can't see how that could happen, we can trust God.

Years ago, I read an article by Emily Perl Kingsley, an advocate for people with disabilities. It is titled "Welcome to Holland," and I think it reveals a powerful truth about expectations.

> *I am often asked to describe the experience of raising a child with a disability – to try to help people who have not shared that unique experience to understand it, to imagine how it would feel. It's like this . . .*
>
> *When you're going to have a baby, it's like planning a fabulous vacation trip—to Italy. You buy a*

bunch of guidebooks and make wonderful plans. The Coliseum. The Michelangelo David. The gondolas in Venice. You may learn some handy phrases in Italian. It's all very exciting.

After months of eager anticipation, the day finally arrives. You pack your bags and off you go. Several hours later, the plane lands. The stewardess comes in and says, "Welcome to Holland." "Holland?!?" you say. "What do you mean Holland?? I signed up for Italy! I'm supposed to be in Italy. All my life I've dreamed of going to Italy."

But there's been a change in the flight plan. They've landed in Holland and there you must stay. The important thing is they haven't taken you to a horrible, disgusting, filthy place full of pestilence, famine and disease. It's just a different place.

So you must go out and buy new guidebooks. And you must learn a whole new language. And you will meet a whole new group of people you never would have met. It's just a different place. It's slower-paced than Italy, less flashy than Italy. But after you've been there for a while and you catch your breath, you look around...and you begin to notice Holland has windmills...and Holland has tulips. Holland even has Rembrandts.

But everyone you know is busy coming and going from Italy...and they're all bragging about what a wonderful time they had there. And for the rest of your life, you will say, "Yes, that's where I was supposed to go. That's what I had planned."

And the pain of that will never, ever, ever, ever go away...because the loss of that dream is a very, very significant loss.

But...if you spend your life mourning the fact that you didn't get to go to Italy, you may never be free to enjoy the very special, the very lovely things... about Holland.

The loss of an expectation hurts. But if all we do is spend our time fixating on what we lost, we'll miss the bigger picture. We'll fail to realize that God wants to work through our unmet expectations to fulfill a purpose even more wonderful than we could imagine. Take your unmet expectation to the Lord and tell Him that you're hurting. But above all, trust Him to work through your pain to bring Him glory.

CHAPTER THREE

A Tale of Two Hearts:
Contrasting the Expectations of
Mary and Judas

As we've followed Mary and Martha throughout the pages of the Gospels, we've learned how to recognize and deal with unmet expectations. But our final glimpse into their home, just days before Jesus would give His life on the cross, teaches us another powerful truth about expectations. In this final encounter, we learn that a heart settled in Christ and fulfilled by Him is a heart freed from damaging expectations.

Imagine what it would be like to have Jesus spend one of His last meals before the cross with you. Mary, Martha, and their brother Lazarus had the opportunity to experience such a dinner. As in the other two occasions we've encountered these two sisters and their brother (in their home and at Lazarus' tomb), Jesus' disciples are also present. But this particular instance highlights one of the disciples: Judas.

You remember Judas—the disciple who eventually betrayed Jesus. Because we associate Judas' name with betrayal, we tend to picture him as a villain-ish character. To properly grasp this story, however, it is important to realize that to any onlooker, including Jesus' other disciples, Judas appeared to be the picture of sincerity and dedication. They trusted him so much that they made him the treasurer of their collective finances (John 12:6) and didn't believe that he was the betrayer of Christ even when Jesus directly told them he was (John 13:26–29). But this story shows us something much deeper than Judas' outward appearance; it reveals what was going on in his heart.

In fact, this story provides a powerful contrast between a heart filled with a personal agenda and unfulfilled expectations (Judas) and a heart filled with gratitude and every expectation fulfilled in Christ (Mary).

> *Then Jesus six days before the passover came to Bethany, where Lazarus was which had been dead, whom he raised from the dead. There they made him a supper; and Martha served: but Lazarus was one of them that sat at the table with him. Then took Mary a pound of ointment of spikenard, very costly, and anointed the feet of Jesus, and wiped his feet with her hair: and the house was filled with the odour of the ointment. Then saith one of his disciples, Judas Iscariot, Simon's son, which should betray him, Why was not this ointment sold for three hundred pence, and given to the poor? This he said, not that he cared for the poor; but because he was a thief, and had the bag, and bare what was put therein. Then said Jesus, Let her alone: against the day of my burying hath she kept this. For the poor always ye have with you; but me ye have not always.*—JOHN 12:1–8

Jesus had recently raised Lazarus from the dead, and public opinion of Christ's ministry shifted afterward. While some recognized this miracle as a powerful proof of Christ's deity, the Pharisees and other religious leaders who didn't want to lose their positions of honor, sought to silence Christ. Tensions were mounting in Jerusalem, and to get away, Jesus returned to Bethany for a quiet evening with His friends. This wasn't a long trip—Bethany was about two miles away from Jerusalem. When the Lord arrived, Martha began serving, and Mary and Lazarus sat at the table with the Lord.

The Lord knew that His time to die for our sins was quickly approaching, and I think Mary grasped this too. She approached this moment as a farewell dinner, sitting at the feet of Jesus and pouring out on Him her most valuable possession—a pound of spikenard ointment. This costly ointment was worth over a year's wages. Given so freely, it was Mary's expression of true love for and worship of Christ.

Once Mary broke the ointment over Jesus' feet, she began to wash his feet with her hair. This was an incredible act of humility. In Jewish culture, women did not unbind their hair in public. Mary was completely broken before her Lord and wanted to show humble reverence to Him.

To Judas, however, what Mary was doing was unthinkable, and he began to forcefully express his disapproval. His heart, in fact, was the direct opposite of Mary's. Notice the contrast between Mary and Judas.

Expectation versus Agenda

We've noted that not all expectations are wrong. God desires that, as His children, we would expect Him to be our faithful Father. He wants us to have our expectations fulfilled in *Him*.

This was Mary's experience. She had loved and followed Christ and had spent much time sitting at His feet and absorbing His words. Her heart was full, and her love overflowed into an act of great sacrifice. Jesus had exceeded Mary's expectations in every way, including raising her brother from the dead. But even more importantly, because she knew Him and valued the spiritual significance of His message, she appreciated the promises that were being fulfilled in Christ.

For Judas, the opposite was true. His expectations had not been met in Christ. This is because Judas didn't have biblically-founded expectations, but his own personal agenda. Like the other disciples, he expected that Jesus would become the political king of the Jews (Luke 19:11) and that he would achieve special prestige when Jesus became king. But unlike the other disciples, when he realized this wasn't happening, he cashed out, betraying Jesus for thirty pieces of silver (Matthew 26:14–16).

The greatest danger of expectations comes when we expect God to do what He never promised to do. If we believe that God's job is to make our lives comfortable and to give us everything we want, when our dreams don't come true, we blame God for the loss and disappointment. For instance, I've known women who have prayed for the healing of a loved one, and when God answered their prayers in a different way than they hoped, they became bitter toward God. Because they expected that God would do something He never promised to do ("obey" their prayers), they were disappointed.

But if our hearts have every expectation surrendered to God and if we are sitting at His feet soaking in His Word and growing in our knowledge of God, we will find every need of our heart fulfilled in Christ.

This is what Paul expressed to the Colossians believers as he wrote, "For this cause we also, since the day we heard it, do not cease to pray for you, and to desire that ye might be filled with the knowledge of his will in all wisdom and spiritual understanding; That ye might walk worthy of the Lord unto all pleasing, being fruitful in every good work, and increasing in the knowledge of God; Strengthened with all might, according to his glorious power, unto all patience and longsuffering with joyfulness; Giving thanks unto the Father, which hath made us meet to be partakers of the inheritance of the saints in light: Who hath delivered us from the power of darkness, and hath translated us into the kingdom of his dear Son: In whom we have redemption through his blood, even the forgiveness of sins" (Colossians 1:9–14).

But there is another element of expectation versus agenda in the contrast of Mary and Judas, and that is Judas' criticism of Mary.

Judas had an expectation of how Mary should spend her money, and he imposed this expectation on Mary. He thought the way she was worshipping the Lord was wrong and that she should have spent her money on more practical means of service. He basically accused her of being wasteful in her worship and neglectful of the poor.

Over the years, I've seen many women who come to Christ and begin to grow in their walk with the Lord and eagerly worship and serve Him. Then, someone, perhaps a family member or friend, comes along and begins to question and accuse them for this worship and service. They say things like, "You shouldn't be going to church so much." "You don't need to give your money to the church." "You shouldn't be sacrificing your time." They don't understand, because they haven't known what it is to be full of love for Christ.

Mary had the right response to Judas' criticism. Instead of answering, she continued worshipping her Saviour. As Mary was anointing the Lord's feet, I have to think that she was reflecting on what the Lord had done for her. She had no real expectation from Jesus; instead, she was surrendered to His will. She remembered what He had taught her. She remembered how following His teaching had changed her life. She remembered how He had raised her brother from the dead. The victories of the past compelled her to worship Christ with total abandon.

I find that it's all too easy to forget what God has done for us. But if we don't take the time to consciously remember victories and blessings in our lives, our worship for Christ will stagnate. One of the most effective ways that I've found to remember what God has done for me is to journal. When I need to be reminded of God's goodness, I flip through that journal and find encouragement to keep serving the Lord even through trials. It realigns my expectations from what I'm hoping the outcome of my current circumstances will be to remembering all that God has already given me.

Are you finding your expectations met in Christ? Or do you have an agenda for what He should be doing in your life? The difference between the two approaches is the difference between a fulfilled walk with God and a constant grasping for something tangible or circumstantial to fill the empty places in your heart.

Gratitude versus Entitlement

While Mary's sacrifice was the outpouring of gratitude, Judas' criticism came from a heart of greed. The Bible specifically tells us his motive for questioning why she hadn't given the money to the poor: "This he said, not that he cared for the poor; but because he was a thief, and had the bag, and bare what was put therein" (John 12:6).

Judas was a thief. If Mary had contributed her money to the poor instead of spending it on spikenard, he would have been able to skim a large commission off the top.

Did Judas believe he deserved what he was stealing? Did he rationalize all he did for Jesus and the work involved in keeping the accounts? I don't know. But I do know that greed had such a hold on Judas that he betrayed Christ for thirty pieces of silver. When Judas realized he wasn't reigning with Christ as a political king of the Jews, he wanted to get what money he could out of Him. Money, it seems, had captivated Judas' full attention and aspirations.

Mary, captivated by gratitude to Christ, was free from any sense of entitlement.

I've often heard the statement, "The foundation of gratitude is the expectation of nothing." While we should have the faith to expect that God will keep His promises, we free our hearts from unfulfilled expectations when we recognize that God doesn't owe us anything.

Gratitude helps us to see what *is* there instead of what is *not* there. If we go through life with an attitude of, "I deserve this," we'll be disappointed when we don't get what we expected. But if we go through life thinking, "Lord, I'm so thankful for whatever You do give to me. I don't deserve anything," we will notice all of the unexpected blessings that God gives us. Lack of gratitude, however, can cause us to place our eyes in the wrong place because we'll always be thinking of what we don't have.

I once read about two old friends who ran into each other. As they were catching up on each other's lives, the one man said to the other, "You look a little depressed."

His friend responded, "You won't believe it, but three weeks ago, my uncle died and left me $10,000."

The first man said, "That's incredible!"

His friend then said, "But you don't understand. Two weeks ago, my cousin died and left me $15,000."

Once again, the first man expressed his surprise. His friend continued, "Last week, my aunt died and left me $20,000."

The first man turned to this friend and said, "I don't get it! Why are you so moody, then?"

The friend glumly responded, "This week, nothing's happened."

We laugh at this story, but there's a real principle involved. Sometimes, when we're continually blessed, we'll develop an expectation. If God blesses us with money, great relationships, or a great job, for example, we start to expect more and more. What's worse is we can stop appreciating all that God has done for us in the first place.

Sometimes as parents we see our children struggle with this, particularly at Christmastime if they have expectations of what they think they should get.

I remember the first Christmas after our family moved to Lancaster, California. The church we had come to serve had told us when we came that they had no money to pay us. We were thankful for the opportunity to serve and have many experiences of God's provision because of it. As that first Christmas approached, I remember struggling with the Lord, knowing there was no money to make our children's Christmas special. In an answer to prayer, a church member generously gave us a present for each of our children. I was so thankful that they would have something to open on Christmas morning.

The next Christmas, the church gave my husband a bonus. With that bonus, my husband and I went to Toys-R-Us and bought as many gifts as we possibly could. I was determined that my children would not have the same experience as they did the prior year.

But on Christmas morning, it was I who was in for a huge disappointment. As soon as my kids ripped open one present, they tossed it to the side and moved on to the next. Instead of taking the time to enjoy the gifts we bought them, they couldn't wait to get to the next one. I sat back and cried, saying, "Last Christmas was the best Christmas ever! This Christmas is the worst Christmas ever!" (I think my husband was convinced that I had lost it, because I'd said almost the same thing the previous year.) I had completely changed my perspective about last Christmas when I saw my children's attitudes. In fact, when my kids got to the last gift, they looked at me and asked, "Where's the next present?" I never forgot that Christmas or the lesson I learned about expectations. When we expect something that God never wanted us to expect, we're setting ourselves up for ingratitude and disappointment.

I look at Mary and all that she had to be thankful for. She was physically able to sit with Jesus—what an incredible opportunity! Jesus chose to visit her family's house during His final days on earth when there were many other places He could have visited. He raised her brother from the dead. Gratitude for all that the Lord had done compelled Mary to express her love to the Lord.

As we seek to cultivate an attitude of gratitude, not expectation, there are three areas for which we should be grateful:

Be grateful for the simple. Too often, we go throughout our day without thinking about the small, simple things around us to be grateful for.

Each year in November, I prepare for the Thanksgiving holiday by writing a list of things I am thankful for each day. Beginning on November 1, I write everything I can think of to give thanks for that begins with the letter A. The next day, I write down all the things I'm thankful for that start with the letter B. In doing so, I find myself remembering gifts God has given me that I might not have noticed before.

I once read that every day, we open up two gifts, and those are our eyes. But how many of us have actually thanked the Lord for them today? I'm thankful that I can walk, that I have food in my refrigerator, and that I have hot coffee in the mornings. I'm thankful for clothes to wear and a warm house. We take so many things for granted without pausing to think about how good God is to us. Yet God deserves our praise and thanksgiving for every blessing in our lives.

Be grateful for the spiritual. If you're a Christian, you have Jesus in your life. What an incredible gift! You have a home in Heaven. You have a Heavenly Father who loves you so much that He died for you. You have a plan specially crafted by God for your life. You have the Bible and the opportunity to take your requests to the Lord in prayer.

It's so easy to wake up, look at our to-do list, and start tackling our day without thanking the Lord for salvation and the spiritual blessings that He has given us. Part of cultivating an attitude of gratitude is seeking to praise God for both the simple and spiritual blessings He has given us.

Be grateful for the sorrowful. Initially, this is not something we think to do. Why would we praise God for something bad that has happened to us? To understand this, look at 1 Thessalonians 5:18. We're told, "In every thing give thanks: for this is the will of God in Christ Jesus concerning you."

In life, we will sometimes walk through unimaginably difficult times. But even in those times, we're commanded to give thanks. We don't have to understand why we're going through what we're going through. But we can trust that God does have a purpose and a plan. We can thank Him for working all things together for our good as He conforms us to the image of Christ: "And we know that all things work together for good to them that love God, to them who are the called according to his purpose. For whom he did foreknow, he also did predestinate to be conformed to the image of his Son…."

One of the most convicting thoughts to me about Mary was her heart of gratitude. She had no expectation of something from the Lord; she was simply thankful to sit at His feet. Instead of having a heart of gratitude, however, Judas had a heart of expectation. He believed he should have gotten more out of following Jesus, and when that didn't happen, He betrayed Christ.

In a world that is so focused on materialism and with a God who so lavishes us with His gracious gifts, we need to be like Mary, not Judas.

Contentment versus Greed

Contentment and gratitude seem similar at first, but they are actually different. Gratitude is being happy with what you *do* have, but contentment is being happy with what you *don't* have. The Bible tells us, "But godliness with contentment is great gain. For we brought nothing into this world, and it is certain we can carry nothing out. And having food and raiment let us be therewith content" (1 Timothy 6:6–8).

The next two verses of this passage contrast contentment with greed. Although they don't mention Judas, they certainly describe him: "But they that will be rich fall into temptation and a snare, and into many foolish and hurtful lusts, which drown men in destruction and perdition. For the love of money is the root of all evil: which while some coveted after, they have erred from the faith, and pierced themselves through with many sorrows" (1 Timothy 6:9–10). Judas' greed led him to steal and betray Christ, and ultimately to suicide (Matthew 27:5).

But to Mary, it was an honor to give back what she had to the One who had given so much to her. Many commentaries I've read suggest that Mary purchased the pound of ointment she gave Christ by using the money of her dowry—the money her parents had set aside for her marriage. This is conjuncture, but here is the reasoning: At no time are Mary, Martha, or Lazarus' parents mentioned in Scripture, so we assume they were likely dead. Furthermore, in Bible times, it was strange for a woman to inherit money from her parents. Therefore, it's likely that Mary's sister, Martha, was previously married and that her siblings now lived with her. Mary may have been unmarried, and to purchase the ointment, she gave up her dowry. In giving up her dowry, she was giving up her dream to be married. This was an incredible act of surrender, and it came from a heart filled with contentment, not a heart grasping for more.

True worship costs. It is an outpouring of love, and love freely gives. We see this in the life of David who when offered a place to make a sacrifice to the Lord at no cost, declined. "And the king said unto Araunah, Nay; but I will surely buy it of thee at a price: neither will I offer burnt offerings unto the Lord my God of that which doth cost me nothing. So David bought the threshingfloor and the oxen for fifty shekels of silver" (2 Samuel 24:24).

One of the marks of contentment, in fact, is sacrifice. If we are always wanting what we don't have, we cling tightly to what we do have, hoping to add to it or to leverage it to gain more. But if we are content with God's gracious gifts, we are surrendered to sacrificially give to God and others.

To Judas, who was full of greed, following Christ had been a disappointment. He didn't get out of it what he had hoped. But to Mary, who was full of contentment, worshipping Christ was a privilege. She couldn't give back enough to show her gratitude for what He had given to her.

It strikes me that both Mary and Judas spent much time with Christ while He was on earth—Judas even more than Mary. Yet because their expectations were different, their ability to experience the fullness of what Christ gives was different as well.

Mary received from Jesus what He gave, while Judas expected what had never been promised.

Mary gave grateful thanks for the blessings of God, while Judas believed he was entitled to more.

Mary was content and thus free to sacrificially give, while Judas greedily took what wasn't his.

This tale of two hearts is also a lesson in two names. *Mary* is a name parents gladly give their girls, while *Judas* is rarely given. Proverbs 10:7 tells us, "The memory of the just is blessed: but the name of the wicked shall rot." Mary is remembered for her devotion to the Lord, but Judas is remembered as a traitor.

The good thing for us is that our stories are still being written. The tale of your heart isn't finished. So if you, like me, want to grow in grateful, contented worship of Christ, take a lesson from Mary, and spend time at the feet of Jesus getting to know Him. *He* is everything you need.

CONCLUSION

Even though Mary and Martha lived two thousand years ago, they faced similar struggles in their expectations as we do today. Martha, like many of us, dealt with an unmet expectation from someone she loved: her sister. Both sisters walked through a difficult death. And they both saw God work an incredible victory in their lives. Later, Mary experienced opposition from others for her sacrificial service to the Lord.

We too deal with expectations both big and small on a daily basis. But if we don't learn how to handle these expectations biblically, the confusion and discouragement that results can be detrimental to our walk with the Lord and our relationships with others. In fact, expectations often reveal more about our hearts than they do about the people around us or circumstances in which we find ourselves. Too often, they reveal pride and entitlement, rather than gratitude and service.

So what about you? Is there a gap between your expectations and reality?

Have you recognized any expectations you have that you hadn't previously identified? Are you communicating them instead of anticipating others will "just know"?

Or perhaps you are struggling with the pain of unmet expectations. Bring your disappointments to the Lord, and ask Him to help you glorify Him through them. He will not only heal your broken heart, but He will give you His peace.

What about in your relationship with the Lord? Are you serving Him out of a heart of grateful, sacrificial worship? Or is there an agenda of something you think you should get out of it?

Ultimately, God desires that our expectations are met in *Him*. This isn't to say that He makes everything we hope for come to pass, but that as we get to know Him better, we find that He is everything we need and *exceeds* our expectations. He is the One who will never let us down.

God always keeps His Word, fulfills His promises, and exceeds our expectations. As we grow in our knowledge of Him and our relationship with Him, we will never be disappointed.

ABOUT THE AUTHOR

TERRIE CHAPPELL and her husband, Paul, have been married since 1980. They live in Lancaster, California, where her husband pastors Lancaster Baptist Church. Terrie leads the ladies ministries, teaches a children's Sunday school class, and serves as an instructor at West Coast Baptist College. She is the author of several books that encourage ladies. The Chappells have four married children, who are all serving in Christian ministry, and ten grandchildren.

For more information about Terrie, please visit terriechappell.com.

OTHER BOOKS BY TERRIE CHAPPELL...

The Choice Is Yours

Life Happens. Walking with God Is a decision.

We live in a culture that caters to our choices. God has given us a much better guide, however, in His Word. Unlike our fickle and untrustworthy opinions, God's Word never changes. In this book, Terrie will lead you through twelve choices that can strengthen or weaken your walk with God.

It's a Wonderful Life

Serving God Joyfully in Marriage and Ministry

From the very first page, your heart will be uplifted by Terrie's candid, humorous, and down-to-earth approach to loving God, supporting your husband, and serving God's people both biblically and joyfully.

Save the Day

Applying God's Wisdom to Life's Struggles

Tucked into a less-known passage of Scripture is the story of an unnamed woman, simply referred to as "a wise woman." In a desperate moment, recorded in 2 Samuel 20, her wisdom saved the day for her hometown, the army of King David, and the entire nation of Israel.

STRIVINGTOGETHER.COM

ALSO AVAILABLE AS EBOOKS